A Quote A Day

by Marc Zirogiannis

Zirogiannis, Marc
A Quote A Day

128 pages

ISBN#: 978-0-359-17292-4

Inquiries or additional information contact:

Marc A. Zirogiannis

Email: tkdlifemagazine@gmail.com

PRINTED IN THE UNITED STATES OF AMERICA

FOR MY BOYS

About the Author

Marc Zirogiannis holds a B.A. from Long Island University and a *Juris Doctor* from Hofstra University's School of Law. Mr. Zirogiannis is a world renowned Business Development Consultant. Mr. Zirogiannis has practiced the martial arts for over 28 years and earned a 3rd Dan under the supervision of Grandmaster Yeon Hwan Park in Levittown, New York. He has been active in meditation for, over 13 years. He has published numerous books on a variety of subjects, and, is currently the Editor in Chief of **Taekwondo Life Magazine**, an international Tae Kwon Do print publication. He lectures on a variety of topics, including suicide prevention, business development, and matters of the martial arts. His last novel, **The Suffering of Innocents,** has won critical acclaim and been the subject of a radio program.

Acknowledgements

Endless thanks for the love and support of my sons, DJ, Deme, Joseph and Sebastian. Without them it all means nothing.

This book is intended to be timeless. There is a quote for every day of the calendar year. There is no correct order to read these quotes; however, the hope is that the reader will find a meaningful quote to inspire them each day.

The best suggested use of this book is to read the daily quote, but more significantly to take some time throughout the day to think about and apply it to the reader's life.

-Marc Zirogiannis

January 1st

"What you leave behind is not what is engraved in Stone monuments, but what is woven into the lives of others."

-Pericles

January 2nd

"If your actions inspire others to dream more, learn more, do more, and become more, you are a leader."

-John Quincy Adams

January 3rd

"Once we accept our limits we go beyond them."

-Albert Einstein

January 4th

"The old adage practice makes perfect is not completely true. Practice makes BETTER for sure, but only PERFECT PRACTICE MAKES PERFECT. Practice badly and perform badly."

-Taekwondo Master

January 5th

"There is no greater gift that you can give to your children than to be mindful in their presence."

-Jon Kabat-Zinn

January 6th

"The seed of speed is in the mind."

-Coach Mick Clegg

January 7th

"Every choice transforms possibility into actuality. The key to creative manifestation is conscious choice making."

-Deepak Chopra

January 8th

"Success is the sum of small efforts, repeated day in and day out."

-R. Collier

January 9th

"Successful people do all the things that unsuccessful people don't want to do."

-John Paul Dejorin

January 10th

"Do not pray for an easy life but the strength to endure a difficult one."

-Bruce Lee

January 11th

"You can not share what you do not have. Therefore, you must find inner peace before you can share it with the world."

-Unknown

January 12th

"For a father to be a good parent he must remember the most you can hope for is the bronze medal."

-Unknown

January 13th

"It is not what you do for your children, but what you have taught them to do for themselves, that will make them successful human beings."

-Ann Landers

January 14th

"Each unit leader must be performing at a high level. If each unit is performing at maximum capacity, then there is no way that the team will lose."

-Urban Meyer

January 15th

"Happiness is when what you think, what you say, and what you do are in harmony."

-Mahatma Gandhi

January 16th

"When you realize how perfect everything is you will tilt your head back and laugh at the sky."

-The Buddha

January 17th

"Strength does not come from winning. Your struggles develop your strengths. When you go through hardships and decide not to surrender, that is strength."

-Arnold Schwarzenegger

January 18th

"The difference between a successful person and others is not a lack of strength, not a lack of knowledge, but rather a lack of will."

-Vince Lombardi

January 19th

"Realize deeply that the present moment is all you ever have."

-Eckhart Tolle

January 20th

"For what shall it profit a man, if gain the whole world, and suffer the loss of his soul?"

-Jesus Christ

January 21st

"Success is not final, failure is not fatal; it is the courage to continue that counts."

-Winston Churchill

January 22nd

"It is not living that matters, but living rightly."

-Socrates

January 23rd

"Realize deeply that the present moment is all you ever have."

-Eckhart Tolle

January 24th

"I am not bound to win, but I am bound to be true. I am not bound to succeed, but I am bound to live by the light that I have. I must stand with anybody that stands right, and stand with him while he is right, and part with him when he goes wrong."

-Abraham Lincoln

January 25th

"When you talk you are only repeating what you already know. When you listen you may learn something new."

-The 14th Dalai Lama

January 26th

"I have learned that courage is not the absence of fear, but the triumph over it."

-Nelson Mandela

January 27th

"The art of being happy lies in the power of extracting happiness from common things."

-Henry Ward Beecher

January 28th

"Love all, trust a few, do wrong to none."

-Shakespeare

January 29th

"No valid plans for the future can be made by those who have no capacity for living now."

-Alan Watts

January 30th

"You can't control how some people will treat you or what they say about you. You can control how you react to it."

-Unknown

January 31st

"Why would you live your life worrying about something that's not going to happen?"

-Bill Parcells

February 1st

"The two most powerful warriors are patience and time."

-Leo Tolstoy

February 2nd

"Stop being afraid of what could go wrong, and start being excited about what could go right."

-Tony Robbins

February 3rd

"When the winds of change blow, some people build walls and others build windmills."

-Ancient Chinese Proverb

February 4th

"Life is a series of natural and spontaneous changes. Don't resist them; that only creates sorrow. Let reality be reality. Let things flow naturally forward in whatever way they like."

-Lao Tzu

February 5th

"I alone cannot change the world, but I can cast a stone across the waters to create many ripples."

-Mother Teresa

February 6th

"Very little is needed to make a happy life; it is all within yourself, in your way of thinking."

-Marcus Aurelius

February 7th

"Family is not an important thing, it's everything."

-Michael J. Fox

February 8th

"It's the friends you can call up at 4 a.m. that matter."

-Marlene Dietrich

February 9th

"Friendship improves happiness, and abates misery, by doubling our joys, and dividing our grief."

-Cicero

February 10th

"I hated every minute of training, but I said 'Don't quit. Suffer now and live the rest of your life as a champion."

-Muhammad Ali

February 11th

"I have decided to stick with love. Hate is too great a burden to bear."

-Dr. Martin Luther King Jr.

February 12th

"In the end our lives are defined by one thing- the quality of our personal relationships."

-Dr. Phillip Goldberg

February 13th

"I've learned that people will forget what you said, people will forget what you did, but people will never forget how you made them feel."

-Maya Angelou

February 14th

"To love is to burn, to be on fire."

-Jane Austen

February 15th

"All you need is love."

-The Beatles

February 16th

"The heart is like a garden: It can grow compassion or fear, resentment or love. What seeds will you plant there?"

-Jack Kornfield

February 17th

"Great things are not accomplished by those who yield to trends and fads and popular opinion."

-Jack Kerouac

February 18th

"This is my simple religion. There is no need for temples; no need for complicated philosophy. Our own brain, our own heart is our temple; the philosophy is kindness."

-The 14th Dalai Lama

February 19th

"There is no such thing as a hopeless situation. Every single circumstance of your life can change!"

-Rhonda Byrne-<u>The Secret</u>

February 20th

"Do not fear mistakes. You will know failure. Continue to reach out."

-Benjamin Franklin

February 21st

"There are better starters than me but I'm a strong finisher."

-Usain Bolt

February 22nd

"Tough times never last, but tough people do."

-Robert H. Schuller

February 23rd

"Realize deeply that the present moment is all you ever have."

-Eckhart Tolle

February 24th

"Great things are not done by impulse, but by a series of small things brought together."

-Vincent Van Gogh

February 25th

"Bravery is the capacity to perform properly even when scared half to death."

-Gen. Omar Bradley

February 26th

"He who has achieved success has worked well, laughed often, and loved much."

-Elbert Hubbard

February 27th

"Correct your mind and the rest of your life will fall into place."

-Lao Tzu

February 28th

"You cannot dream yourself into a character; you must hammer and forge yourself one."

-James Anthony Froude

February 29th (Leap Years)

"All that we are is the result of what we have thought."

-The Buddha

March 1st

"The question isn't who is going to let me; it's who is going to stop me."

-Ayn Rand

March 2nd

"Honesty is the first chapter in the book of wisdom."

-Thomas Jefferson

March 3rd

"Try not to become a man of success, but rather try to become a man of value."

-Albert Einstein

March 4th

"A good commander is benevolent and unconcerned with fame."

-Sun Tzu

March 5th

"Choose a job you love, and you will never have to work a day in your life."

-Confucius

March 6th

"It's not what you look at that matters, it's what you see."

-Henry David Thoreau

March 7th

"Facing it, always facing it, that's the way to get through. Face it."

-Joseph Conrad

March 8th

"Most everything that you want is just outside your comfort zone."

-Jack Canfield

March 9th

"It is in your moments of decision that your destiny is shaped."

-Tony Robbins

March 10th

"The key to immortality is first living a life worth remembering."

-Bruce Lee

March 11th

"Do you really want to be happy? You can begin by being appreciative of who you are and what you've got."

-Benjamin Hoff

March 12th

"I seek not to know the answers, but to understand the questions."

-David Carradine

March 13th

"If you don't know where you are going, you'll end up someplace else."

-Yogi Berra

March 14th

"The euphoria of winning isn't saying, 'I won.' The euphoria of winning is to hug your teammate and say, 'We have found a way to accomplish something."

-Urban Meyer

March 15th

"You must not lose faith in humanity. Humanity is an ocean; if a few drops of the ocean are dirty, the ocean does not become dirty."

-Mahatma Gandhi

March 16th

"Holding on to anger is like grasping a hot coal with the intent of throwing it at someone else; you are the one who gets burned."

-The Buddha

March 17th

"The mind is the limit. As long as the mind can envision the fact that you can do something, you can do it, as long as you really believe 100 percent."

-Arnold Schwarzenegger

March 18th

"Leaders are made, they are not born. They are made by hard effort, which is the price which all of us must pay to achieve any goal that is worthwhile."

-Vince Lombardi

March 19th

"The primary cause of unhappiness is never the situation but your thoughts about it."

-Eckhart Tolle

March 20th

"Practice being the kind of person you wish to attract."

-Wayne Dyer

March 21st

"A pessimist sees the difficulty in every opportunity; an optimist sees the opportunity in every difficulty."

-Winston Churchill

March 22nd

"Prayer must lead us beyond mind, words, and ideas to a more spacious place where God has a chance to get in."

-Father Richard Rohr

March 23rd

"Education is the most powerful weapon which you can use to change the world."

-Nelson Mandela

March 24th

"It is far better to be alone, than to be in bad company."

-George Washington

March 25th

"The goal is not to be better than the other man, but your previous self."

-The 14th Dalai Lama

March 26th

"Love makes your soul crawl out from its hiding place."

-Zora Neale Hurston

March 27th

"Life isn't about finding yourself. Life is about creating yourself."

-George Bernard Shaw

March 28th

"People grow through experience if they meet life honestly and courageously. This is how character is built."

-Eleanor Roosevelt

March 29th

"People never learn anything by being told, they have to find out for themselves."

-Paulo Coehlo

March 30th

"Given the choice between the experience of pain and nothing, I would choose pain."

-William Faulkner

March 31st

"Life is 10% what happens to us and 90% how we react to it."

-Dennis P. Kimbro

April 1st

"We are what we repeatedly do. Excellence, then, is not an act, but a habit."

-Aristotle

April 2nd

"Be yourself, everyone else is already taken."

-Oscar Wilde

April 3rd

"The secret of getting ahead is getting started."

-Mark Twain

April 4th

"The man who says he can, and the man who says he can not…they are both correct."

-Confucius

April 5th

"The only man who never makes mistakes is the man who never does anything."

-Theodore Roosevelt

April 6th

"There is no friend as loyal as a good book."

-Ernest Hemingway

April 7th

"The highest levels of performance come to people who are centered, intuitive, creative, and reflective-people who see a problem as an opportunity."

-Deepak Chopra

April 8th

"Your attitude, not your aptitude, will determine your altitude."

-Zig Ziglar

April 9th

"The key to successful leadership today is influence, not authority."

-Ken Blanchard

April 10th

"Love is all we have, the only way that each can help the other."

-Euripides

April 11th

"Think in the morning. Act in the noon. Eat in the evening. Sleep in the night."

-William Blake

April 12th

"It is easier to build strong children than to repair broken men."

-Frederick Douglass

April 13th

"All our dreams can come true if we have the courage to pursue them."

-Walt Disney

April 14th

"The best and most beautiful things in the world cannot be seen or even touched -- they must be felt with the heart."

-Helen Keller

April 15th

"Live as if you were to die tomorrow. Learn as if you were to live forever."

-Mahatma Gandhi

April 16th

"Be patient with yourself. Self-growth is tender; it's holy ground. There's no greater investment."

-Stephen Covey

April 17th

"Many of life's failures are people who did not realize how close they were to success when they gave up."

-Thomas A. Edison

April 18th

"In a word, never let go on these three things: Faith, Hope, and Love. And know that the greatest of these will always be love."

-St. Paul

April 19th

"A champion is someone who gets up when he can't."

-Jack Dempsey

April 20th

"I've learned that something constructive comes from every defeat."

-Coach Tom Landry

April 21st

"Courage is what it takes to stand up and speak. Courage is also what it takes to sit down and listen."

-Winston Churchill

April 22nd

"The greatest wisdom is knowing that you know nothing."

-Socrates

April 23rd

"I have learned over the years that when one's mind is made up, this diminishes fear; knowing what must be done does away with fear."

-Rosa Parks

April 24th

"Don't cry because it's over. Smile because it happened."

-Dr. Suess

April 25th

"Patience is the mark of true love. If you truly love someone, you must be more patient with that person."

-Thich Nhat Hanh

April 26th

"Injustice anywhere is a threat to justice everywhere."

-Dr. Martin Luther King Jr.

April 27th

"Someone's sitting in the shade today because someone planted a tree a long time ago."

-Warren Buffet

April 28th

"To thine own self be true, and it must follow, as the night the day, thou canst not then be false to any man."

-Shakespeare

April 29th

"You change your life by changing your heart."

-Max Lucado

April 30th

"One man practicing sportsmanship is far better than a hundred men teaching it."

-Coach Knute Rockne

May 1st

"You are what you believe in. You become that which you believe you can become."

-Bhagavad Gita

May 2nd

"Never discourage anyone who continually makes progress, no matter how slow."

-Plato

May 3rd

"There is no coming to consciousness without pain."

-Carl Jung

May 4th

"Life is not always a matter of holding good cards, but sometimes it's about playing a poor hand well."

-Jack London

May 5th

"Note that this journey is uniquely yours, no one else's. So the path has to be your own. You cannot imitate somebody else's journey and still be true to yourself."

-Jon Kabat-Zinn

May 6th

"It's hard to beat a person that never gives up."

-Babe Ruth

May 7th

"Looking at beauty in the world is the first step to purifying the mind."

-Amit Ray

May 8th

"Meditation practice isn't about trying to throw ourselves away and become something better. It's about befriending who we already are."

-Pema Chodron

May 9th

"The groundwork of all happiness is health."

-James Leigh Hunt

May 10th

"Don't confuse having a career with having a life."

-Hillary Rodham Clinton

May 11th

"The first step towards change is awareness. The second step is acceptance."

-Nathaniel Branden

May 12th

"You have to get up every morning with determination if you are to go to bed with satisfaction."

-George Lorimer

May 13th

"Some men see things as they are and ask why. Others dream things that never were and ask why not."

-George Bernard Shaw

May 14th

"Your time is limited. Don't waste it trying to live someone else's life."

-Steve Jobs

May 15th

"All you need is love, but a little chocolate now and then doesn't hurt."

-Charles M. Schulz

May 16th

"Success is nothing more than few simple disciplines practiced every day."

-Jim Rohn

May 17th

"No individual has any right to come into the world and go out of it without leaving behind distinct and legitimate reasons for having passed through it."

-George Washington Carver

May 18th

"Defeat is a state of mind; no one is ever defeated until defeat has been accepted as a reality."

-Bruce Lee

May 19th

"You can only lose what you cling to."

-The Buddha

May 20th

"When we get too caught up in the busy-ness of the world we lose connection with one another -and with ourselves."

-Jack Kornfield

May 21st

"I have never let schooling interfere with my education."

-Mark Twain

May 22nd

"Practice is all that stands between you and everything."

-Rhonda Byrne

May 23rd

"I am not the smartest fellow in the world, but I can sure pick smart colleagues."

-Franklin Delano Roosevelt

May 24th

"If you develop the habits of success, you will make success a habit."

-Michael Angier

May 25th

"Amateurs sit and wait for inspiration, the rest of us get up and go to work."

-Stephen King

May 26th

"Education is the passport to the future, for tomorrow belongs to those who prepare for it today."

-Malcolm X

May 27th

"Champions aren't made in gyms. Champions are made from something they have deep inside of them-a desire, a dream, a vision. They have to have the skill, and the will, but the will must be stronger than the skill."

-Muhammad Ali

May 28th

"Believe and you are halfway there."

-Theodore Roosevelt

May 29th

"No one who ever gave their best ever regretted it."

-George Halas

May 30th

"Never spend your money before you have it."

-Thomas Jefferson

May 31st

"There are times when we must risk everything, including life itself, for those basic American ideals of freedom, justice, and equality, without which this land cannot survive."

-Greek Orthodox Archbishop Jakovos

June 1st

"We are products of our past, but we don't have to be prisoners of it."

-Pastor Rick Warren

June 2nd

"That which does not kill us makes us stronger."

-Friedrich Nietzsche

June 3rd

"Happiness is the meaning and the purpose of life, the whole aim and end of human existence."

-Aristotle

June 4th

"Change is the law of life. Those who look only to the past or present are certain to miss the future."

-John F. Kennedy

June 5th

"There is nothing impossible to him who will try."

-Alexander the Great

June 6th

"It is a common experience that a problem difficult at night is resolved in the morning after the committee of sleep has worked on it."

-John Steinbeck

June 7th

"Self-awareness is not just relaxation and not just meditation. It must combine relaxation with activity and dynamism."

-Deepak Chopra

June 8th

"My religious practice is stillness and kindness."

-Oprah Winfrey

June 9th

"Now that the Barn's burnt down I can see the moon."

-Zen poet

June 10th

"An early morning walk is a blessing that lasts the whole day."

-Henry David Thoreau

June 11th

"You never know what is enough unless you know what is more than enough."

-William Blake

June 12th

"Sitting still is a way of falling in love with the world and everything in it."

-Pico Iyler

June 13th

"Freedom consists not in doing what we like, but in having the right to do what we ought to."

-Pope John Paul II

June 14th

"Life is not a problem to be solved, but a reality to be experienced."

- Søren Kierkegaard

June 15th

"There is nothing permanent except change."

- Heraclitus

June 16th

"Time is the wisest of all things that are; for it brings everything to light."

-Thales of Miletus

June 17th

"A good teacher opens the door for you, but you must enter the room by yourself."

-Old Zen Saying

June 18th

"Do not let your fire go out. Do not let the hero in your soul perish in the lonely frustration for the life you deserved but were never able to reach. The world you desired can be won. It exists. It is real. It is possible. It can be yours."

-Ayn Rand

June 19th

"Facing it — always facing it — that's the way to get through."

-Joseph Conrad

June 20th

"Your willingness to look at your darkness is what empowers you to change."

-Iyanla Vanzant

June 21st

"In quietness are all things answered."

-A Course in Miracles

June 22nd

"There is only one way to succeed in anything and that is to give everything. I do and I demand that my players do. Any man's finest hour is when he has worked his heart out in a good cause and lies exhausted on the field of battle... victorious."

-Vince Lombardi

June 23rd

"How people treat you is their Karma; how you react is yours."

-Wayne W. Dyer

June 24th

"Life is a tragedy when seen up in a close-up, but a comedy in the long-shot."

-Charlie Chaplin

June 25th

"One day, in retrospect, the years of struggle will strike you as the most beautiful."

-Sigmund Freud

June 26th

"Discipline is the habit of taking consistent action until one can perform with unconscious competence. Discipline weighs ounces but regret weighs tons."

-Grandmaster Jhoon Rhee

June 27th

"The truth is the kindest thing we can give folks in the end."

-Harriet Beecher Stowe

June 28th

"The fault, dear Brutus, is not in our stars, but in ourselves."

-Shakespeare

June 29th

"How wonderful it is that nobody need wait a single moment before starting to improve the world."

-Anne Frank

June 30th

"Do your little bit of good where you are; it's those little bits of good put together that overwhelm the world."

-Bishop Desmond Tutu

July 1st

"It is true that integrity alone won't make you a leader, but without integrity you will never be one."

-Zig Ziglar

July 2nd

"Our character is what we do when we think no one is looking."

-H. Jackson Brown, Jr.

July 3rd

"If you do what you have always done, you'll get what you have always gotten."

-Tony Robbins

July 4th

"Failure, repeated failures, are finger posts on the road to achievement. One fails forward toward success."

-C.S. Lewis

July 5th

"To be true to ourselves, we must be true to others."

-Jimmy Carter

July 6th

"There are only two days in the year that nothing can be done. One is called yesterday and the other is called tomorrow. Today is the right day to Love, Believe, Do, and mostly Live."

-The 14th Dalai Lama

July 7th

"Wherever your heart is, there you will find your treasure."

-Paulo Coelho

June 8th

"Your talent is God's gift to you. What you do with it is your gift back to God."

-Leo Buscaglia

July 9th

"When you eliminate the impossible, whatever remains, however improbable, must be the truth."

-Sir Arthur Conan Doyle

July 10th

"Knowing is not enough, we must apply. Willing is not enough, we must do."

-Bruce Lee

July 11th

"Don't bend; don't water it down; don't try to make it logical; don't edit your own soul according to the fashion. Rather, follow your most intense obsessions mercilessly."

-Franz Kafka

July 12th

"Life is the sum of all your choices."

-Albert Camus

July 13th

"Three things cannot be long hidden: the sun, the moon, and the truth."

-The Buddha

July 14th

"Stop living in the world of 'what if' and start living in the world of 'what is'."

-Dr. Stephen Morand

July 15th

"When you learn, teach. When you get, give."

-Maya Angelou

July 16th

"The most precious gift we can offer to others is our presence. When mindfulness embraces those we love, they will bloom like flowers."

-Thich Nhat Hanh

July 17th

"There are no shortcuts—everything is reps, reps, reps."

-Arnold Schwarzenegger

July 18th

"If you trust yourself, any choice you make will be correct. If you do not trust yourself, anything you do will be wrong."

-David Carradine

July 19th

"Only those who dare to fail greatly can ever achieve greatly."

-Robert F. Kennedy

July 20th

"When everything goes wrong, what a joy to test your soul and see if it has endurance and courage!"

-Zorba The Greek

July 21st

"God gave us two ears but only one mouth for a reason."

-Unknown

July 22nd

"Do in your heart what you feel to be right because you will be criticized anyway."

-Eleanor Roosevelt

July 23rd

"Don't worry that children never listen, worry that they are always watching you."

-Robert Fulghum

July 24th

"Although the world is full of suffering, it is also full of the overcoming of it."

-Helen Keller

July 25th

"It's not the will to win that matters-everyone has that. It's the will to prepare to win that matters."

-Bear Bryant

July 26th

"If you aren't going all the way, why go at all?"

-Joe Namath

July 27th

"Cowards never start. The weak never finish. Winners never quit."

-Unknown

July 28th

"Successful people maintain a positive focus in life no matter what is going on around them."

-Jack Canfield

July 29th

"Intelligence without ambition is like a bird without wings."

-Salvador Dali

July 30th

"Whether you think you, or you think you can't, you are probably right."

-Henry Ford

July 31st

"People rarely succeed unless they have fun in what they are doing?"

-Dale Carnegie

August 1st

"Those who dare to fail miserably can achieve greatly."

-John F. Kennedy

August 2nd

"There is only one way to avoid criticism: Say Nothing. Do Nothing. Be Nothing."

-Aristotle

August 3rd

"Every child is an artist. The problem is staying an artist when you grow up."

-Pablo Picasso

August 4th

"Leaders are those that always empower others."

-Bill Gates

August 5th

"To drop into being means to recognize your interconnectedness with all life, and with being itself. Your very nature is being part of larger and larger spheres of wholeness."

-Jon Kabat-Zinn

August 6th

"Out of clutter find simplicity. From discord find harmony. Amidst difficultly find opportunity."

-Albert Einstein

August 7th

"Don't judge each day by the harvest you reap but by the seeds you plant."

-Robert Louis Stevenson

August 8th

"The only thing necessary for evil to triumph is for good men to do nothing."

-Edmund Burke

August 9th

"There is only one corner of the universe you can be certain of improving, and that's your own self."

-Aldous Huxley

August 10th

"Act as if what you do makes a difference. It does."

-William James

August 11th

"The journey of a thousand miles begins with one step."

-Lao Tzu

August 12th

"Happiness resides not in possessions, and not in gold. Happiness dwells in the soul."

-Democritus

August 13th

"If opportunity doesn't knock, build a door."

-Milton Berle

August 14th

"Think in the morning. Act in the noon. Eat in the evening. Sleep in the night."

-William Blake

August 15th

"Tell me and I forget. Teach me and I remember. Involve me and I learn."

-Benjamin Franklin

August 16th

"A leader is one who knows the way, goes the way, and shows the way."

-John C. Maxwell

August 17th

"No act of kindness, no matter how small, is ever wasted."

-Aesop

August 18th

"That's what I consider true generosity: You give your all, and yet you always feel as if it costs you nothing."

-Simone de Beauvoir

August 19th

"Life's most persistent and urgent question is 'What are you doing for others?'"

-Martin Luther King Jr.

August 20th

"The soul is healed by being around children"

-Fyodor Dostoyevsky

August 21st

"A little bit of mercy makes the world less cold and more just."

-Pope Francis

August 22nd

"Nothing can stop the man with the right mental attitude from achieving his goal; nothing on earth can help the man with the wrong mental attitude."

-Thomas Jefferson

August 23rd

"Spread love everywhere you go. Let no one ever come to you without leaving happier."

-Mother Teresa

August 24th

"Above all, be the heroine (or hero) of your life, not the victim."

-Nora Ephron

August 25th

"Strive not to be a person of success but a person of value."

-Albert Einstein

August 26th

"A life is not important except in the impact it has on other lives."

-Jackie Robinson

August 27th

"Before you are a leader success is all about growing yourself. When you become a leader success is all about growing others."

-Jack Welch

August 28th

"Make the most of yourself by fanning the tiny, inner sparks of possibility into flames of achievement."

-Golda Meir

August 29th

"The important thing is this: to be able, at any moment, to sacrifice what we are for what we could become."

-Maharishi Mahesh Yogi

August 30th

"Obstacles are things a person sees when he takes his eyes off his goal."

-E. Joseph Cossman

August 31st

"Perfection is not attainable, but if we chase perfection we can catch excellence."

-Vince Lombardi

September 1st

"Step out of the history that is holding you back. Step into the new story you are willing to create."
-Oprah Winfrey

September 2nd

"Those who have no time for healthy eating will sooner or later have to find time for illness."

-Edward Stanley

September 3rd

"Do what you have to until you can do what you want to."

-Oprah Winfrey

September 4th

"Your relationship with others are always a direct reflection of the relationship you have with yourself."

-Michael Thomas Sunnarborg

September 5th

"In my experience, each failure contains the seeds of your next success-if you are willing to learn from it."

-Paul Allen

September 6th

"The only limit to the height of your achievements is the reach of your dreams and your willingness to work them."

-Michelle Obama

September 7th

"Our life is shaped by our mind, for we become what we think."

-The Buddha

September 8th

"A leader takes people where they want to go. A great leader takes people where they don't necessarily want to go, but ought to be."

-Roslyn Carter

September 9th

"Nearly all men can stand adversity, but if you want to test a man's character, give him power."

-Abraham Lincoln

September 10th

"In matters of style, swim with the current; in matters of principle, stand like a rock."

-Thomas Jefferson

September 11th

"To be persuasive we must be believable; to be believable we must be credible; credible we must be truthful."

-Edward R. Murrow

September 12th

"Learning never exhausts the mind."

-Leonardo da Vinci

September 13th

"It's not what we get, but who we become, what we contribute, that gives meaning to our lives."

-Tony Robbins

September 14th

"Time is a precious commodity. I refuse to allow what little time I have to be contaminated by self-pity, anxiety, or boredom."

-Max Lucado

September 15th

"As a general rule, a reputation is built on manner as much as on achievement."

-Joseph Conrad

September 16th

"The greatest danger for most of us is not that our aim is too high and we miss it, but that it is too low and we reach it."

-Michelangelo

September 17th

"Drink your tea slowly and reverently, as if it is the axis on which the world earth revolves – slowly, evenly, without rushing toward the future."

-Thich Nhat Hahn

September 18th

"Motivation is what gets you started. Habit is what keeps you going."

-Jim Ryun

September 19th

"The next time you feel slightly uncomfortable with the pressure in your life, remember no pressure, no diamonds. Pressure is a part of success."

-Eric Thomas

September 20th

"Never confuse a single defeat with a final defeat."

-F. Scott Fitzgerald

September 21st

"We can't help everyone, but we can help someone."

-Ronald Reagan

September 22nd

"A wise man never knows all, only the fool knows everything."

-African Proverb

September 23rd

"In helping others we shall help ourselves, for whatever good we give out completes the circle and comes back to us."

-Flora Edwards

September 24th

"When you bow, you should just bow; when you sit, you should just sit; when you eat, you should just eat."

-Shunryu Suzuki

September 25th

"The will to win, the desire to succeed, the urge to reach your full potential... these are the keys that will unlock the door to personal excellence."

-Confucius

September 26th

"If it doesn't challenge you it won't change you."

-Unknown

September 27th

"Take criticism seriously, but not personally. If there is truth or merit in the criticism, try to learn from it. Otherwise, let it roll right off you."

-Hillary Rodham Clinton

September 28th

"Be polite to all, but intimate with few."

-Thomas Jefferson

September 29th

"The truth you believe and cling to makes you unavailable to hear anything new."

-Pema Chodron

September 30th

"Many receive advice, only the wise profit from it."

-Harper Lee

October 1st

"The higher we are placed, the more humbly we should walk."

-Marcus Tullius Cicero

October 2nd

"I am here to serve. I am here to inspire. I am here to love. I am here to live my truth."

-Deepak Chopra

October 3rd

"Humankind has not woven the web of life. We are but one thread within it. Whatever we do to the web, we do to ourselves. All things are bound together. All things connect."

-Chief Seattle, Duwamish

October 4th

"My life is my message."

-Mahatma Gandhi

October 5th

"The first to apologize is the bravest. The first to forgive is the strongest. The first to forget is the happiest."

-Unknown

October 6th

"Life is full of misery, loneliness, and suffering – and it's all over much too soon."

-Woody Allen

October 7th

"Vision without execution is hallucination."

-Henry Ford

October 8th

"Prepare for the unknown by studying how others in the past have coped with the unforeseeable and the unpredictable."

-George S. Patton

October 9th

"Fear regret more than failure."

-Taryn Rose

October 10th

"Adversity is the best teacher."

-Old Russian Saying

October 11th

"Without continual growth and progress, such words as improvement, achievement, and success have no meaning."

-Benjamin Franklin

October 12th

"Every great dream begins with a dreamer. Always remember, you have within you the strength, the patience, and the passion to reach for the stars to change the world."

-Harriet Tubman

October 13th

"Courage is contagious. When a brave man takes a stand, the spines of others are often stiffened."

-Rev. Billy Graham

October 14th

"I attribute my success to this - I never gave or took any excuse."

-Florence Nightingale

October 15th

"Each day of our lives we make deposits in the memory banks of our children."

-Charles R. Swindoll

October 16th

"Do not take the agenda that someone else has mapped out for your life."

-John C. Maxwell

October 17th

"The life of a man consists not in seeing visions and in dreaming dreams, but in active charity and in willing service."

-Henry Wadsworth Longfellow

October 18th

"Luck is what happens when preparation meets opportunity."

-James A. Michener

October 19th

"It is better to ask some questions than to know all the answers."

-James Thurber

October 20th

"Within all of us is a divine capacity to manifest and attract all that we need and desire."

-Dr. Wayne Dyer

October 21st

"One of the best ways to persuade others is with your ears-by listening to them."

-Dean Rusk

October 22nd

"Research your own experience. Absorb what is useful, reject what is useless, and add what is specifically your own."

-Dan Inosanto

October 23rd

"Confidence comes from victory, but strength comes from struggle."

-Arnold Schwarzenegger

October 24th

"Within all of us is a divine capacity to manifest and attract all that we need and desire."

-Will Rogers

October 25th

"What you have been taught by listening to others' words you will forget quickly; what you have learned with your whole body you will remember for your life."

-Gichin Funakoshi

October 26th

"Within all of us is a divine capacity to manifest and attract all that we need and desire."

-Bertrand Russell

October 27th

"Once you replace negative thoughts with positive ones, you'll start having positive results."

-Willie Nelson

October 28th

"If you do not change direction, you may end up where you are heading."

-Lao Tzu

October 29th

"You must tell yourself, no matter how hard it is, or how hard it gets I'm going to make it."

-Les Brown

October 30th

"When we are no longer able to change a situation - we are challenged to change ourselves."

-Viktor E. Frankl

October 31st

"Courage is being scared to death... and saddling up anyway."

-John Wayne

November 1st

"When you arise in the morning think of what a precious privilege it is to be alive, to breathe, to think, to enjoy, to love."

-Marcus Aurelius

November 2nd

"The only impossible journey is the one you never begin."

-Tony Robbins

November 3rd

"Character, simply stated, is doing what you say you're going to do."

-Hyrum W. Smith

November 4th

"Anger is an acid that can do more harm to the vessel in which it is stored than to anything on which it is poured."

-Mark Twain

November 5th

"Ability is what you're capable of doing. Motivation determines what you do. Attitude determines how well you do it."

-Lou Holtz

November 6th

"Motivation is the art of getting people to do what you want them to do because they want to do it."

-Dwight D. Eisenhower

November 7th

"It is impossible to begin to learn that which one thinks one already knows."

-Epictetus

November 8th

"Forgiveness is a virtue of the brave."

-Indira Gandhi

November 9th

"You cannot have a positive life and a negative mind."

-Joyce Meyer

November 10th

"March on. Do not tarry. To go forward is to move toward perfection. March on, and fear not the thorns, or the sharp stones on life's path."

-Khalil Gibran

November 11th

"Adversity is the first path to truth."

-Lord Byron

November 12th

"A genuine leader is not a searcher for consensus but a molder of consensus."

-Martin Luther King Jr.

November 13th

"Success is no accident. It is hard work, perseverance, learning, studying, sacrifice and most of all, love of what you are doing or learning to do."

-Pele'

November 14th

"If you put off everything till you're sure of it, you'll never get anything done."

-Norman Vincent Peale

November 15th

"Start by doing what's necessary; then do what's possible; and suddenly you are doing the impossible."

-Francis of Assisi

November 16th

"In order to heal others, we first need to heal ourselves. And to heal ourselves, we need to know how to deal with ourselves."

-Thich Nhat Hanh

November 17th

"Perfection is attained by slow degrees; it requires the hand of time."

-Voltaire

November 18th

"We need to realize that our path to transformation is through our mistakes. We're meant to make mistakes, recognize them, and move on to become unlimited."

-Yehuda Berg

November 19th

"Who you spend your time with will have a great impact on what kind of life you live. Spend time with the right people."

-Joel Osteen

November 20th

"Experience is the teacher of all things."

-Julius Caesar

November 21st

"You can have intelligence, you can have connections, you can have opportunities fall out of the sky. But in the end, hard work is the true, enduring characteristic of successful people."

-Marsha Evans

November 22nd

"Know thyself."

-Socrates

November 23rd

"I am the greatest, I said that even before I knew I was."

-Muhammad Ali

November 24th

"Winners are not afraid of losing. But losers are. Failure is part of the process of success. People who avoid failure also avoid success."

-Robert Kiyosaki

November 25th

"The way to get started is to quit talking and begin doing."

-Walt Disney

November 26th

"Doing nothing can sometimes be the most effective form of action."

-Kevin Kwan

November 27th

"Success comes from curiosity, concentration, perseverance and self-criticism."

-Albert Einstein

November 28th

"I can't imagine a person becoming a success who doesn't give this game of life everything he's got."

-Walter Cronkite

November 29th

"Success comes when people act together; failure tends to happen alone."

-Deepak Chopra

November 30th

"Focusing your life solely on making a buck shows a poverty of ambition. It asks too little of yourself. And it will leave you unfulfilled."

-Barack Obama

December 1st

"If you set your goals ridiculously high and it's a failure, you will fail above everyone else's success."
-James Cameron

December 2nd

"The first principle of success is desire – knowing what you want. Desire is the planting of your seed."

-R. Collier

December 3rd

"Optimism is the faith that leads to achievement."

-Helen Keller

December 4th

"The great secret of true success, of true happiness, is this: the man or woman who asks for no return, the perfectly unselfish person, is the most successful."

- Swami Vivekananda

December 5th

"Success is a journey, not a destination. The doing is often more important than the outcome."

-Arthur Ashe

December 6th

"Most of the successful people I've known are the ones who do more listening than talking."

-Bernard Baruch

December 7th

"One secret of success in life is for a man to be ready for his opportunity when it comes."

-Benjamin Disraeli

December 8th

"Talent is a gift, but character is a choice."

-John C. Maxwell

December 9th

"The only thing you have 100 percent control over is you."

-Hyrum W. Smith

December 10th

"When I get ready to talk in front of people, I spend two thirds of the time thinking what they want to hear and one third thinking about what I want to say."

-Abraham Lincoln

December 11th

"Follow the three R's-Respect for self-Respect for others-Responsibility for all your actions."

-The Dalai Lama

December 12th

"Every single minute matters, every single child matters, every single childhood matters."

-Kailash Satyarthi

December 13th

"Continuous effort - not strength or intelligence - is the key to unlocking our potential."

-Liane Cordes

December 14th

"Effort without talent is a depressing situation... but talent without effort is a tragedy."

-Mike Ditka

December 15th

"The will to win is important, but the will to prepare is vital."

-Joe Paterno

December 16th

"The place to improve the world around us is first in one's own heart and head and hands."

-Robert M. Pirsig

December 17th

"Everything that happens to you is a form of instruction if you pay attention."

-Robert Greene

December 18th

"The successful warrior is the average man, with laser-like focus."

-Bruce Lee

December 19th

"The foolish reject what they see, not what they think; the wise reject what they think, not what they see."

-Huang Po

December 20th

"An awakened person is someone who finds freedom in good fortune and bad."

-Bodhidharma

December 21st

"In war, as in life, it is often necessary, when some cherished scheme has failed, to take up the best alternative open, and if so, it is folly not to work for it with all your might."

-Winston Churchill

December 22nd

"Take time to be kind and to say 'thank you.'"

-Zig Ziglar

December 23rd

"Determine to live life with flair and laughter."

-Maya Angelou

December 24th

"When the conscious mind expands to embrace deeper levels of thinking, the thought wave becomes more powerful and results in added energy and intelligence."

-Maharishi Mahesh Yogi

December 25th

"A new command I give you: Love one another. As I have loved you, so you must love one another."

-Jesus Christ

December 26th

"Without patience we will learn less in life. We will see less. We will hear less. Ironically, rush and more usually means less."

-Mother Teresa

December 27th

"When you think you can't, revisit a previous triumph."

-Jack Canfield

December 28th

"Enthusiasm is common. Endurance is rare."

-Angela Duckworth

December 29th

"Do not be afraid of your difficulty. Turn toward it. Learn to lean into the wind. Hold your ground."

-Jack Kornfeld

December 30th

"Too often we... enjoy the comfort of opinion without the discomfort of thought."

-John F. Kennedy Jr.

December 31st

"Push yourself again and again. Don't give an inch until the final buzzer sounds."

-Larry Bird